Introduction

'... should develop the connections that pupils make between multiplication and division with fractions and decimals ... demanding efficient mental methods of calculation.'

Upper Key Stage 2 National Curriculum Programme of Study

'The teacher created a positive climate for learning in which pupils were interested and engaged.'

OFSTED Inspector

Welcome to a world of mathematical fun and games!

Easy to play and requiring only basic equipment, these educational games engage even the most reluctant of learners whilst boosting confidence for all.

Great for teachers, intervention workers, teaching assistants, private tutors and parents, the flexible nature of this game pack offers:

▶ practice for specific objectives from the new National Curriculum

▶ a great resource to:
   "ensure students are engaged in learning and generate high levels of commitment to learning"
   (Outstanding Grade Descriptors, *Ofsted School Inspection Handbook* (updated 2014))

▶ the opportunity to demonstrate a commitment to:
   "the social development of pupils at the school" within curriculum time
   (Ofsted Framework for School Inspection (updated 2014))

▶ an effective assessment tool

▶ the promotion of problem solving and thinking skills through game strategy

▶ fun homework activities

Playing Information

All these games require a pack of playing cards and most also need some kind of coloured counters or other objects such as beads or buttons. Suitable materials are available from Tarquin - see page 40 for details. When the picture cards are used the jack represents number eleven, the queen is number twelve and the king is thirteen. To help children remember this you may want to consider writing the actual numbers in the corners of each card.

And that's all you need to know to enjoy years of happy gaming!

David Smith

Duel

Focus

Duel is a game for two players which practices recall and use of facts for multiplication tables up to 12 x 12.

What you need

- Playing cards (kings removed)
- Counters (a different colour for each player)
- Duel game board

How to play

When the kings have been removed from the pack the remaining cards are mixed up and placed in a pile, face-down and within reach of all the players. Each player starts with eight counters, a different colour for each player. Player 1 turns over a card and multiplies that number by any number of their choosing from one up to twelve.

For example

If Player 1 turns over a seven then they can say 7 x 5 = 35 or 7 x 8 = 56. However, they can't calculate 7 x 9 = 63 as that number is not on the game board. If they say the correct answer they can then place their counter on the matching number on the game board.

Play passes to Player 2 and continues in this fashion. If an incorrect answer is given the player can't place a counter on that turn. Players continue to take turns and place their counters on the board. If there is no number on the board that matches a possible answer then that player can turn over another card.

How to win

When all of their counters have been used, players stop turning cards and play a game of draughts to decide the winner. Players are allowed to move and jump over other counters in any diagonal direction. One or more counters can be captured on each move, as shown in the diagram below. The player with the least number of counters on the board moves first and play is limited to two minutes to decide the winner. If there are still counters on the board after two minutes the winner is the player with the most counters remaining.

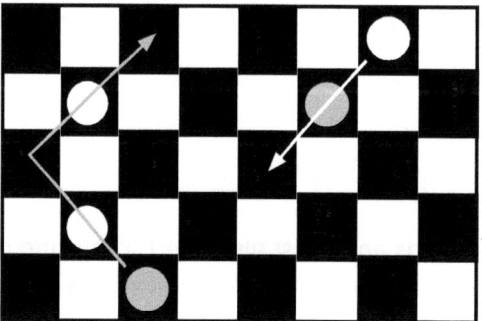 

Rule changes / Next steps

- When a player moves a counter onto a new square, or jumps over another counter to land on a new square, they must say a multiplication fact that would give that answer. If incorrect, they can't move a counter on that turn. This is also the same if a player wants to jump over another counter.
- Play Duel Multiples by multiplying the value of the card by any multiple of ten up to one hundred and twenty before placing a counter on the matching answer on the game board.

ACE Mathematics Games 6

15 exciting activities to engage ages 10–11
David Smith

3. **Introduction**

4. **Duel**
   recall and use facts for
   multiplication tables up to 12 x 12

7. **Hexums**
   recall and use facts for
   multiplication tables up to 12 x 12

10. **Total Tables**
    recall and use facts for
    multiplication tables up to 12 x 12

13. **Square Up**
    recall and use facts for multiplication tables
    up to 12 x 12 and identify factors of numbers
    up to 200

16. **Multiple Madness**
    identify multiples and factors of
    numbers up to 150

18. **Robot Wars**
    identify common factors in
    numbers up to 100

20. **Hooked!**
    use negative numbers and calculate intervals
    across zero

22. **Dare!**
    add and subtract numbers to
    two decimal places

24. **Speed Seekers**
    add and subtract numbers to
    two decimal places

26. **Double Double Cross**
    double and halve numbers to
    one and two decimal places

28. **Battle Squares**
    divide by 100 and add and subtract numbers
    to two decimal places

31. **Tower Power**
    use a range of efficient mental methods with
    numbers up to 100

32. **End of the Line**
    use a range of efficient mental methods with
    numbers up to 150

34. **Quads**
    use a range of efficient mental methods with
    numbers up to 10 000 and to
    one decimal place

36. **Monster Mash-Up!**
    use a range of efficient mental methods with
    numbers up to 10 000 000 and to
    three decimal places

tarquin

Acknowledgements

Thanks are due to many people but especially to my lovely wife and also my dear mum who between them patiently played all the games with me to test their initial suitability. I also have to thank the teachers and children of Peel Park Primary School for giving them a road test, spotting my errors and making suggestions on how they could be further developed and improved. Finally thanks go to the staff at Tarquin, for their support in the editing process.

Dedication

This book is dedicated to the memory of Maxine Firth, an inspirational friend and colleague who shared my ideal of an enjoyment of mathematics for all.

Published by Tarquin Publications
Suite 74, 17 Holywell Hill
St Albans
AL1 1DT

www.tarquingroup.com

Copyright © David Smith, 2014
ISBN: 978-1-907-55090-4

Distributed in the USA by Parkwest
www.parkwestpubs.com
www.amazon.com & major retailers

Distributed in Australia by OLM www.lat-olm.com.au

All rights reserved. Sheets may be copied singly for use by the purchaser only, or for class use under a valid school or institutional licence from the relevant Copyright Licensing society.

Printed and designed in the United Kingdom

DUEL MULTIPLES

350		200		30		560	
	990		1320		700		50
210		450		220		180	
	300		70		360		1100
480		160		1210		550	
	110		630		640		270
1440		240		150		800	
	600		1080		720		140

Hexums

Focus

Hexums is a game for two or three players which practices recall and use of facts for multiplication tables up to 12 x 12.

What you need

▶ Playing cards (kings removed)
▶ Counters (a different colour for each player)
▶ Hexums game board

How to play

When the kings have been removed from the pack the remaining cards are shuffled and placed in a pile, face-down and within reach of all the players. Player 1 turns over a playing card from the pack and places it face-up in front of them. The value of the card is multiplied by ten and can then be multiplied by any chosen multiple of ten from ten to one hundred and twenty.

For example

Player 1 turns over a seven and multiplies it by ten to make seventy. They could then say 70 x 80 = 5600, 70 x 60 = 4200 or 70 x 110 = 7700, as all these answers have a matching number on the game board. They could not, however, say 70 x 120 = 8400, as that number is not on the board. After saying a correct answer Player 1 can place a counter on any of the matching answers on the game board.

Player 2 then turns over a card and multiplies it by ten. They then multiply this number by any multiple of ten from ten to one hundred and twenty. This time a five is turned over and Player 2 says 50 x 50 = 2500, placing a counter on that number on the board.

Play continues in this fashion. If a player gives an incorrect answer they are not able to place a counter on that turn.

How to win

Each player has to try and make a continuous line of coloured counters on adjacent numbers from the outer ring to the inner ring of shaded hexagons, as shown in the diagram.

Rule changes / Next steps

▶ Limit the players to ten counters each to try and get a winner.
▶ To play Hexums Decimals, the value of each turned card is multiplied by any multiple of one tenth from 0.1 up to 1.2.
▶ Record multiplication facts on paper or a whiteboard. At the end of the game use these to generate other multiplication and division facts (as below) and then test each other.

70 x 80 = 5600	so	80 x 70 = 5600	5600 ÷ 70 = 80	and	5600 ÷ 80 = 70
4 x 0.6 = 2.4	so	0.6 x 4 = 2.4	2.4 ÷ 4 = 0.6	and	2.4 ÷ 0.6 = 4

Hexums Mega Multiples

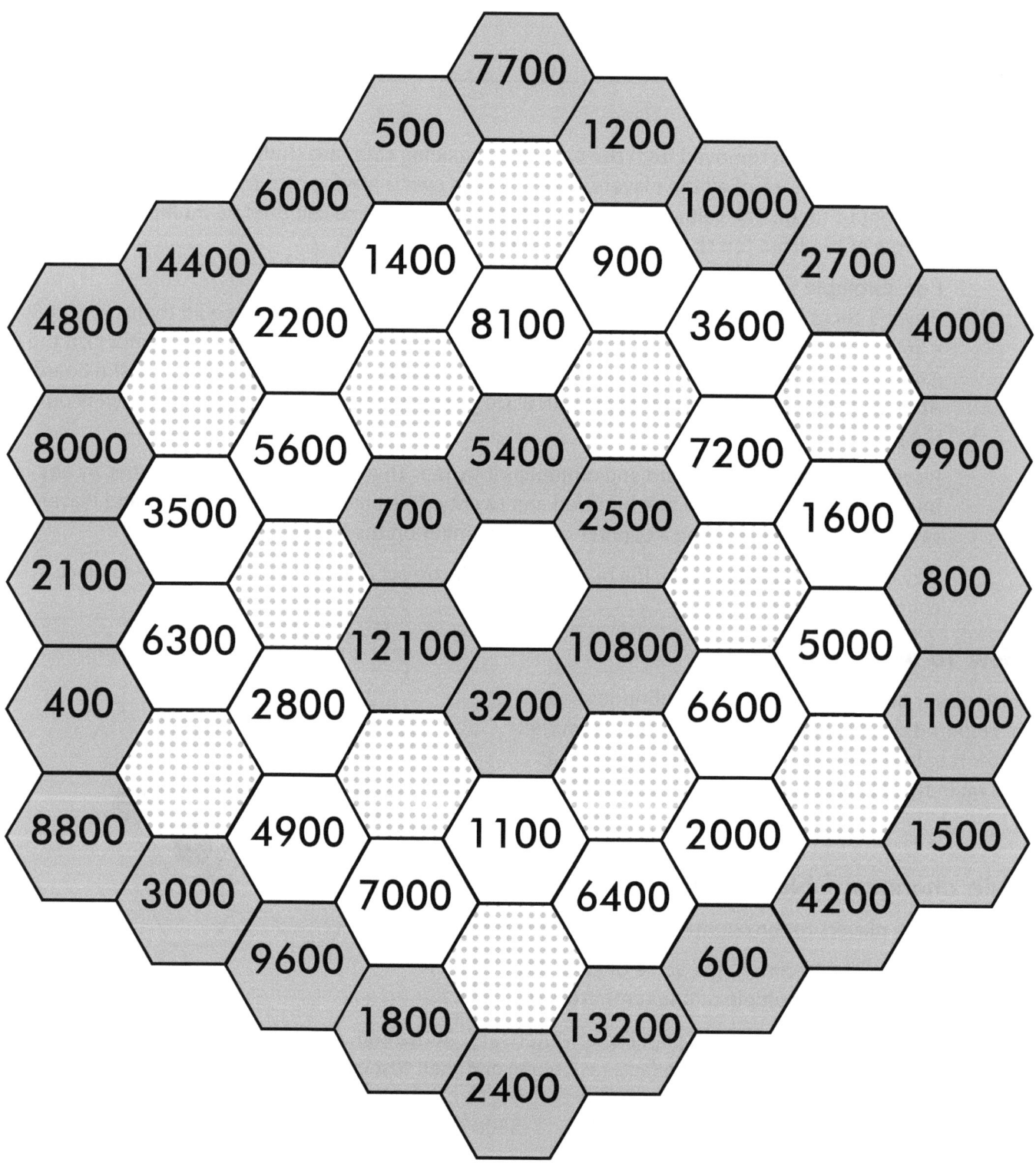

Hexums
Decimals

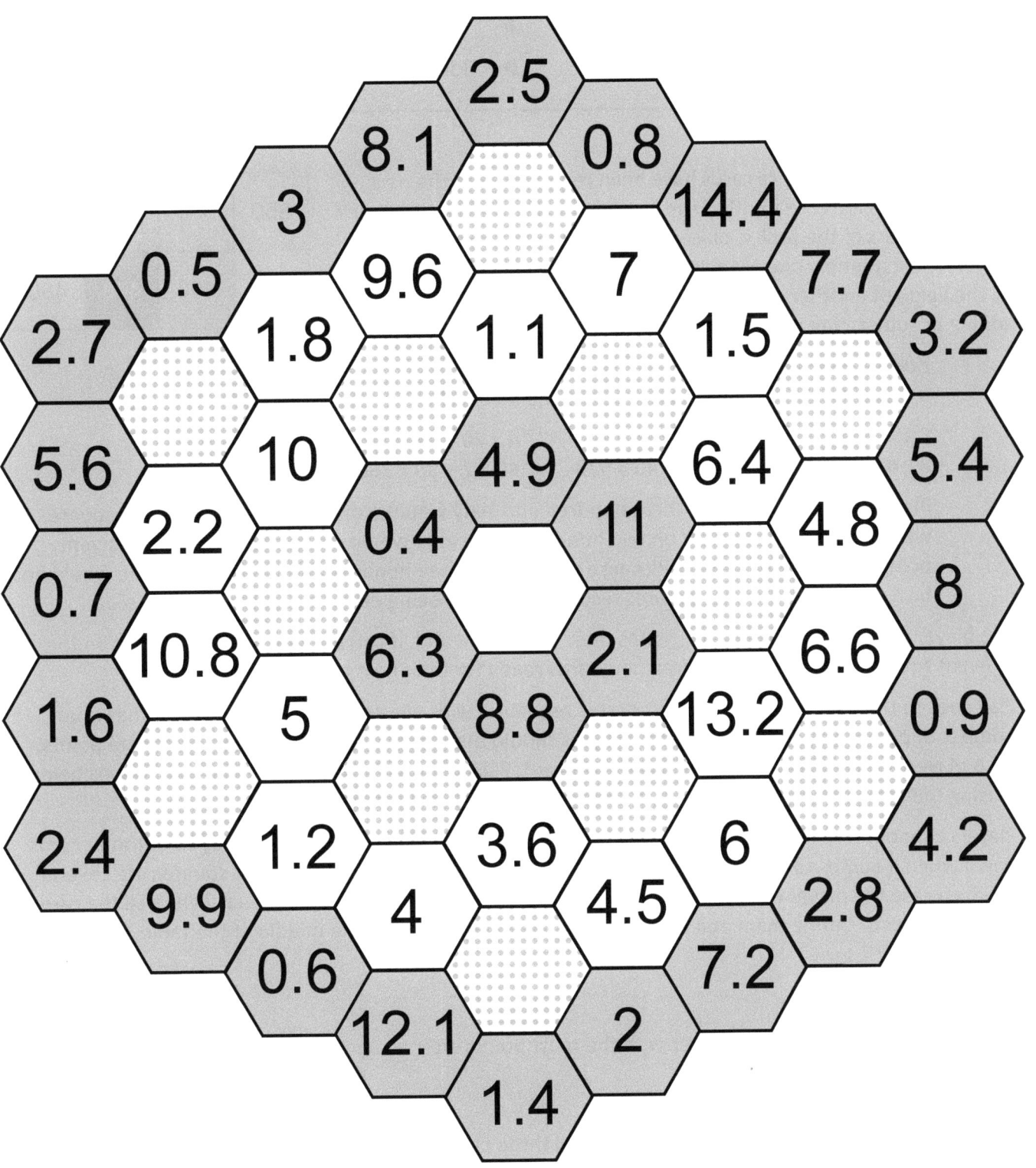

Total Tables

Focus

Total Tables is a game for two or more players which practices recall and use of multiplication facts up to 12 x 12.

What you need

▶ Playing cards (tens and picture cards removed)
▶ Counters (a different colour for each player)
▶ Total Tables game board
▶ Total Tables scorecard

How to play

When the tens and picture cards have been removed from the pack, the remaining cards are shuffled and Player 1 deals three cards to each player. The rest of the pack is placed face-down within reach of all. Players must multiply one of their cards by ten and then multiply this by the value of another card. They then have the extra option of either adding or subtracting the value of the third card multiplied by ten.

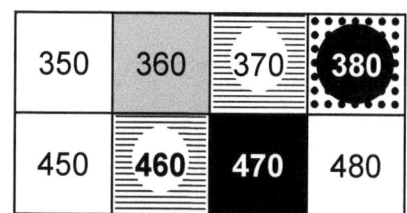

For example

If Player 1 turns over an eight, a seven and a four, they could make the following totals:

8 x 40 = 320	8 x 70 = 560	4 x 70 = 280	80 x 4 + 70 = 390
8 x 40 - 70 = 250	80 x 7 - 40 = 520	40 x 7 + 80 = 360	4 x 70 - 80 = 200

Placing a counter on total three hundred and sixty would score sixty points for a grey square, whereas placing a counter on two hundred and eighty would score one hundred and twenty points for a striped square. Placing a counter on three hundred and twenty, however, would not be a good idea, as dotty squares result in 90 points being deducted from a player's score.

The player places their cards down, states their calculation and, if correct, places their counter on the relevant square. They then draw three new cards ready for their next turn.

Play goes to the next player and the process is repeated, with players trying to achieve the maximum number of points possible on each turn. Players should beware dotty squares, which lose them points. Each player keeps their own score using a scorecard. Players must do all their mental calculations before placing their counter and must also give a correct answer in order to do so.

Players cannot place a counter on a square that is already covered and must be ready to put their cards down when it comes to their turn. Players must place a counter unless all possible squares are covered, in which case the player cannot place a counter but draws three new cards as usual. When all the cards have been used, shuffle them and place them in a pile, face down in the middle of the table, ready for the next player's turn.

How to win

The winner of the game is the player with the most points after an agreed number of rounds.

Rule changes / Next steps

▶ Allow players to multiply the numbers on all three cards, such as 20 x 3 x 6 = 360.
▶ Include the picture cards to produce some more difficult calculations, or remove the aces so that there is no multiplying by one.

Total Tables

10	20	30	40	50	60	70	80	90	
110	120	130	140	150	160	170	180	190	T
210	220	230	240	250	260	270	280	290	A
310	320	330	340	350	360	370	380	390	B
410	420	430	440	450	460	470	480	490	L
510	520	530	540	550	560	570	580	590	E
610	620	630	640	650	660	670	680	690	S
710	720	730	740	750	760	770	780	790	
810	820	830	840	850	860	870	880	890	
		T	O	T	A	L			1000

Full colour game board and scorecards downloadable from www.tarquingroup.com.

Total Tables Scorecard

☐ = 30 points   ■ = 200 points   ▤ = 120 points

▨ = 60 points   ▦ = -90 points

Keep your score like this:

Round Number	Points for square	Total Game points
1	stripes, 120 points	120
2	dotty, -90	120 - 90 = 30
3	grey, 60	30 + 60 = 90

Round Number	Points for square	Total Game points
1		
2		
3		
4		
5		
6		
7		
8		
9		
10		
11		
12		
13		
14		
15		

Square Up

Focus

Square Up is a game for two to four players which practices recall and use of facts for multiplication tables up to 12 x 12 and identifying factors of numbers up to two hundred.

What you need

▶ Playing cards (kings removed)
▶ Counters (a different colour for each player)
▶ Square Up game board

How to play

When the kings have been removed from the pack the remaining cards are shuffled and placed in a pile, face-down and within reach of all the players. Player 1 turns over a playing card from the pack and places it face-up in front of them. The value of the card is then multiplied by any chosen number to one decimal place from zero point three to one point two. The chosen calculation must have a matching answer on the game board on which the player then places their counter.

For example

Player 1 turns over an eight so could say 8 x 0.7 = 5.6, 8 x 1 = 8 or 8 x 0.4 = 3.2, since all these answers have a matching number on the game board. After saying the correct answer to their chosen calculation, Player 1 places a counter on the matching answer.

Player 2 then turns over a card and follows the same procedure. This time a four is turned over so Player 2 says 4 x 0.7 = 2.8 and places their counter on the board.

Players continue to take cards in turn, multiply the value of the card by any number to one decimal place from zero point three to one point two, and place their counters on the board. If a player gives an incorrect answer they are not able to place a counter on that turn. A player may turn over another card if no matching answer can be found on the game board.

How to win

Players have to make the shape of a square, by placing counters on each corner, as shown in the diagram. The square can be any size and in any orientation; the first player to complete one is the winner.

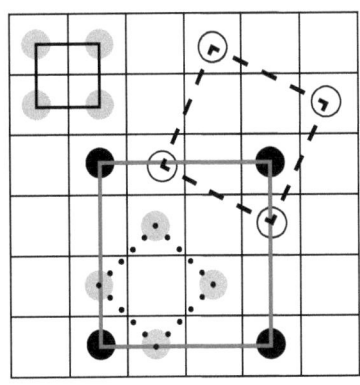

Rule changes / Next steps

▶ To play Square Up Multiples the aces and twos remain out of the pack but the kings can be used. The value of the card turned can be multiplied by any number from three to thirteen. Players must explain how they know the number they are placing is actually a multiple of their card. They can do this by saying things like 8 x 12 = 96 or by counting up in multiples of twelve. Opponents can challenge explanations, and use a calculator to check whether it is correct.

▶ Players score four points for each square they make and play can continue until all their counters have been used or until there are no spaces left on the game board.

SQUARE UP DECIMALS

5.4	0.9	10.8	0.4	3.2	2.5
3.6	5.5	4.2	9.6	12.1	7.2
13.2	10	5.6	0.5	9	3.5
8	0.6	2.8	6	0.8	2.1
1.5	2	14.4	0.7	4.5	9.9
11	4.8	6.6	8.4	12	0.3

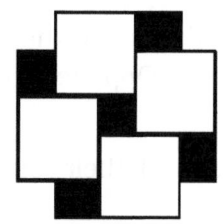
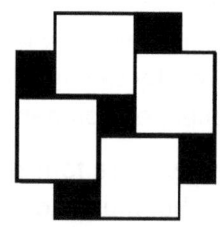

Game Board © Tarquin Photocopiable under licence – for terms see page 2

SQUARE UP MULTIPLES

52	108	70	61	117	55
36	162	25	144	50	121
91	47	88	110	156	64
56	96	169	57	72	90
140	65	23	98	105	136
16	100	49	112	33	154

Game Board © Tarquin Photocopiable under licence – for terms see page 2

Multiple Madness

Focus

Multiple Madness is a game for two or more players which practices identifying multiples and factors of numbers up to 150.

What you need

- ▶ Playing cards (aces to sevens)
- ▶ Counter
- ▶ Multiple Madness game board
- ▶ Whiteboard / paper and pen
- ▶ Calculator

How to play

The cards are shuffled and placed in a pile, face-down and within reach of all the players. Place a counter on the one hundred position in the middle of the game board. Player 1 takes two cards from the top of the pack and multiplies them together to get a total. That player can then move the counter the same number of places on the board by either adding or subtracting from one hundred. Their choice of move depends on the number of points they can score, as follows:

For example

Player 1 picks a four and a two so they can move the counter to position one hundred and eight or ninety-two. One hundred and eight is a multiple of nine so scores nine points, whereas ninety-two is a multiple of four so scores four points. Therefore, Player 1 decides to move the counter to one hundred and eight on the game board and starts their scoring with nine points.

Player 2 then takes two cards, multiplies them together and also adds or subtracts the total from the number under the counter on the game board. Player 2 turns over a five and a nine so has a choice of calculating 108 + 45 = 153 or 108 − 45 = 63. One hundred and fifty-three is not on the game board so Player 2 has to move to sixty-three. This is a multiple of three, seven and nine, so Player 2 claims nine points to add to their score.

Play continues in this fashion. Players can earn points for multiples from three up to twelve but must claim their points and explain how they know the number they have landed on is actually a multiple of that number. For example, fifty-four is a multiple of three (3 points) but the player could show that it is a multiple of nine (9 points). They can do this by saying things like 9 x 6 = 54, 54 ÷ 9 = 6 or even count up in multiples of nine to show that there really are six lots of nine in fifty-four. Their opponent can challenge an explanation and use a calculator to check whether it is correct.

Players keep a running total of their points using a whiteboard or paper and pen. This may be done by someone acting as a scorer / referee, who also decides whether player explanations are good enough to award points.

How to win

The first player to reach a total of fifty points is the winner.

Rule changes / Next steps

- ▶ Allow points for multiples up to fifteen, such as seventy-eight being a multiple of thirteen as 6 x 13 = 78 or one hundred and five being a multiple of fifteen as 7 x 15 = 105. The winning total could then be raised to one hundred points.

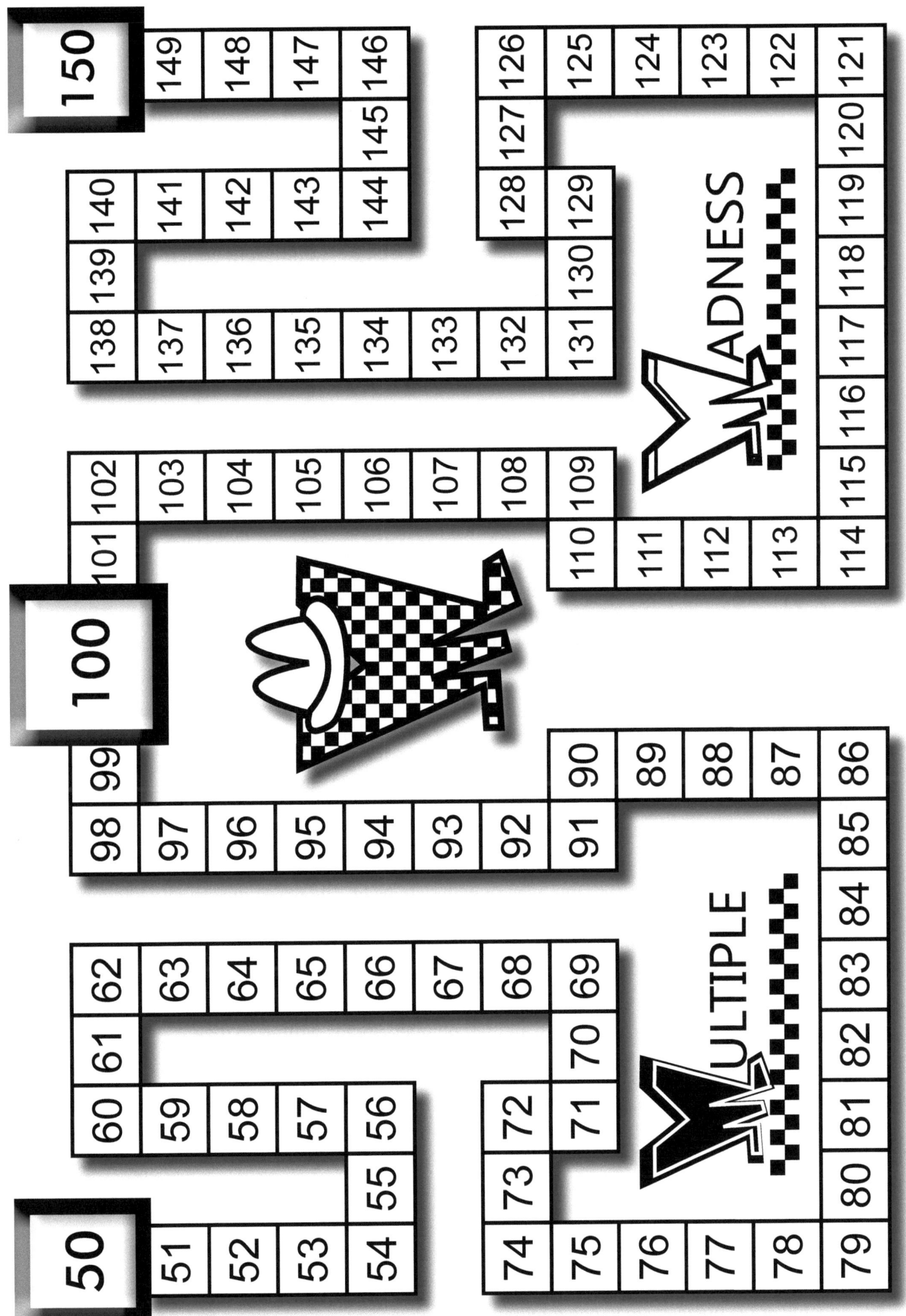

Robot Wars

Focus

Robot Wars is a game for two or more players which practices identifying common factors of numbers up to 100.

What you need

▶ Playing cards (tens & picture cards removed)
▶ Counters (a different colour for each player)
▶ Robot Wars game board

How to play

When the tens and picture cards have been removed from the pack, the remaining cards are shuffled and placed face-down, within reach of all players. Player 1 turns over two cards and puts them together to make a two-digit number. They then write this number in one of the squares on the game board. So if Player 1 turns over a five and a nine they can write fifty-nine or ninety-five. Player 1 decides to write ninety-five.

Player 2 then turns over two cards, a six and an eight. They need to try and make a number that shares a common factor of three or above with a number on the board. The factors of sixty-eight above two are 4, 17, 34 and 68 but none of these are a factor of ninety-five (5, 19 and 95). Therefore, the number has to be written on another empty square on the board, that is not adjacent to ninety-five.

Player 3 then turns over two cards, a three and an ace. Again Player 3 is unable to make a number (thirteen or thirty-one) that shares a common factor above two as another number on the board so their chosen number has to be written on another empty square. Numbers that do not share common factors above two cannot be written in an adjacent square unless it is the only option left on the board.

The next player turns over a five and a two. Twenty-five (5 and 25) shares a factor with ninety-five, whilst fifty-two (4, 13, 26 and 52) shares a factor with sixty-eight. The player may choose either of these options. They chose to write fifty-two next to sixty-eight, stating that these numbers have a common factor of four. Both numbers are then covered with coloured counters. As this player was able to place counters they get another turn.

Players continue to take cards in turn and write their numbers on the board, trying to make a number that shares a factor of three or above with another number already written so they can cover them with counters of their own colour. When all the cards have been used, mix them up and place them back down in a pile within reach of all the players. Play continues until all the squares on the board have been used.

How to win

The winner is the player with the most counters on the game board.

Rule changes / Next steps

▶ Identify prime numbers up to one hundred.

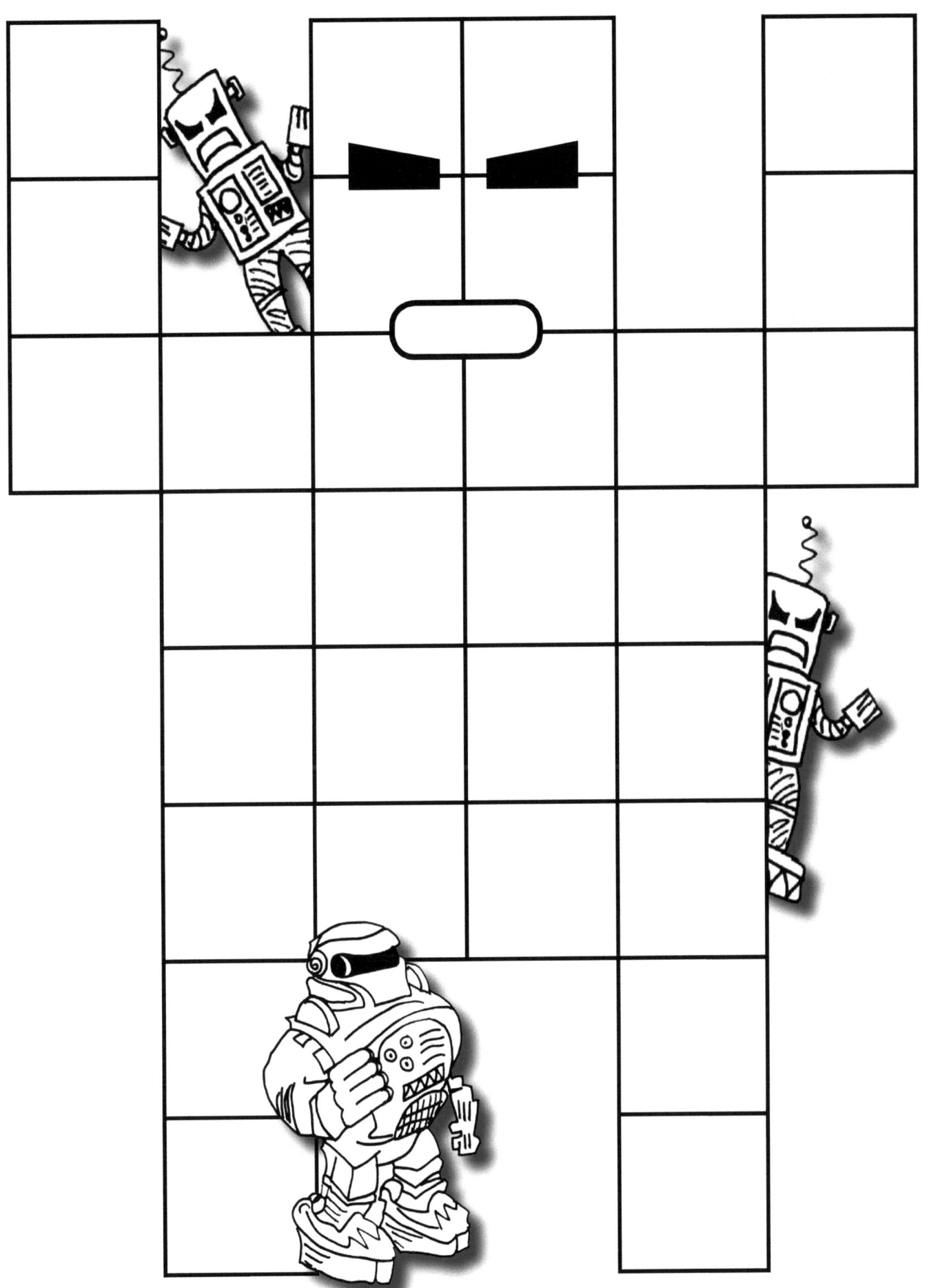

Hooked!

Focus
Hooked! is a game for two players which practices using negative numbers and counting intervals across zero.

What you need
▶ Playing cards
▶ Counter
▶ Hooked! game board

How to play
The cards are shuffled and placed in a pile, face-down between both players. Decide who is counting forwards and who is counting backwards. The player counting forwards moves from left to right along the game board and the player counting backwards moves from right to left. Place a counter on the middle number of the game board.

For example
Player 1 (forwards) turns over a card, doubles its value and then adds the total to the number underneath the counter. If Player 1 turns over a six they double it to twelve, calculate $0 + 12 = 12$, and move the counter to that space on the board. If Player 1 gives an incorrect answer then the counter remains in the same place.

Player 2 (backwards) then turns over a card, doubles its value and subtracts this total from the number underneath the counter. So if Player 2 turns over an eight, they double it to sixteen and then calculate $12 - 16 = {^-}4$, moving the counter to that space on the board.

Players must do all their mental mental calculations before moving the counter. A correct answer must be given in order to move. When all the cards have been used, shuffle them and place them back down in a pile so that play can continue.

How to win
Player 2 (subtracting) hooks the fish and wins by getting the counter to land on or go past minus thirty whilst Player 1 (adding) hooks the fish and wins by getting the counter to land on or go past thirty.

Rule changes / Next steps
▶ Change roles and play again so both players practice their addition and subtraction skills.
▶ Play for a set number of turns and the player who is closest to their end of the game board wins.
▶ Allow players to do the calculation whilst moving the counter at the same time but only when crossing zero.

Dare!

Focus

Dare is a game for two or more players which practices adding and subtracting numbers to two decimal places.

What you need

▶ Playing cards

▶ Counters (a different colour for each player)

▶ Dare! game board

How to play

Firstly, the cards are shuffled and placed in a pile, face-down and within reach of all the players. The players' counters are placed on the number one on the game board, which is the starting position. Player 1 takes a card and doubles its value. They must then divide this total by one hundred and subtract the answer from the value underneath their counter. If correct, they move their counter to the relevant number on the game board.

For Example

Player 1 picks up a six. They double it (to twelve), and then calculate 12 ÷ 100 = 0.12 and then 1 − 0.12 = 0.88). Having found the correct answer, they move their counter to 0.88 on the gameboard.

After moving their counter, Player 1 must then decide whether to play safe, stop and pass the cards to the next player or to 'dare' and turn over another card. If Player 1 decides to dare and turn over another card then:

▶ if the card is the same colour they can continue their turn by performing the necessary calculation (doubling the value on the card, dividing it by one hundred and subtracting it from the number under their counter, in this case 0.88);

▶ if the card is a different colour they must go back to the first grey **DARE SQUARE** they reach by moving backwards along the game board.

If Player 1 decides to stop then play goes to Player 2. Play continues with players taking a card, doubling its value, dividing by one hundred and subtracting this from the number underneath their counter.

Players are encouraged to do all their mental calculations before moving the counter. If a player lands on top of another counter, the counter landed on is moved back to the start or the first **DARE SQUARE** they reach by moving backwards along the game board, (whichever is agreed by the players before play).

How to win

The first player to land on or go past zero (the finish line) is the winner.

Rule changes / Next steps

▶ Remove the lower number cards (1—4) for practice subtracting larger numbers.

▶ Play as an addition game, starting at zero and adding up to the finish line.

▶ Each player starts with a blue dare counter and is allowed to use it once at any time during the game. The dare counter forces another player to dare and carry on even when they have decided to stop. The dared player *must* then carry on for two more cards.

Instruction Sheet © Tarquin Photocopiable under licence – for terms see page 2

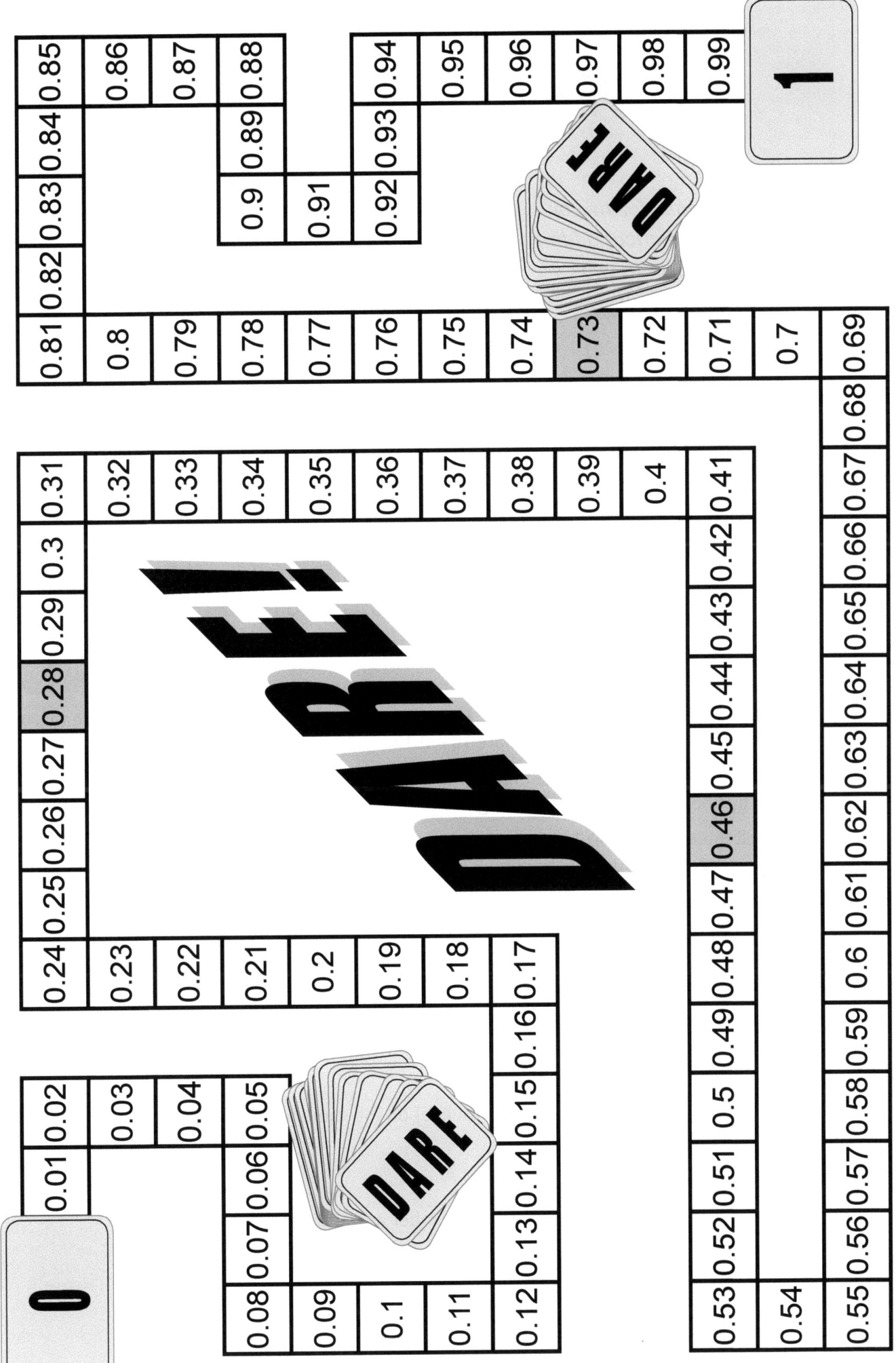

Speed Seekers

Focus

Speed Seekers is a game for two or more players which practices adding and subtracting numbers to two decimal places.

What you need

- Playing cards (eights and higher removed)
- Counters (a different colour for each player)
- Speed Seekers game board
- Calculator (optional)

How to play

The higher cards are removed from the pack and the remainder are shuffled and placed in a pile, face-down and within reach of all the players. Player 1 takes a card from the top of the pack and mulitplies it by three to get a total. They then divide that total by one hundred, subtract their answer from the number underneath their counter on the board, and move their counter to this new position.

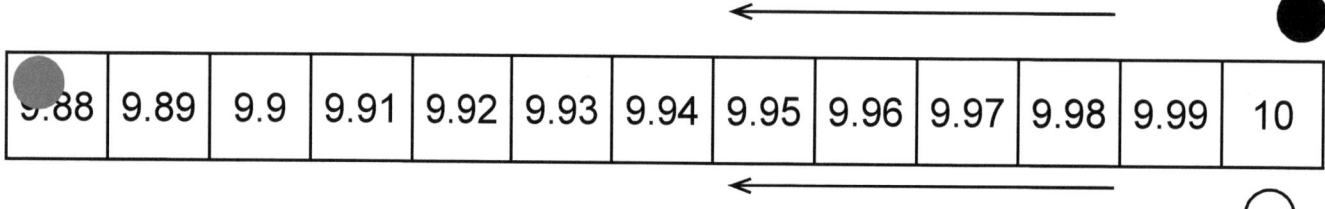

For example

Player 1 (grey counter) turns over a four. First of all they calculate 3 x 4 = 12. They divide this by one hundred (12 ÷ 100 = 0.12), calculate 10 – 0.12 = 9.88, and move their counter accordingly.

Play goes to Player 2, and play continues with players taking cards, multiplying by three, then dividing by one hundred and subtracting this total from the number underneath their counter.

Players must do all their mental calculations before moving their counter. The player must also give the correct answer to move their counter otherwise it remains where it is on the game board.

If a player lands on a Speed Seeker (grey) square they can choose to either move another nine spaces (0.9) or move any one other player backwards nine squares (0.9) on the game board.

If a player lands on top of another counter, the counter landed on is moved back to the first Speed Seeker square they reach by moving backwards along the game board.

How to win

The first player to land on or go past zero (the finish line) on the game board is the winner.

Rule changes / Next steps

- Play as an addition game, starting at the lower number and adding up to the finish line.

Speed Seekers

9 — **10**

9.01, 9.02, 9.03, 9.04, 9.05, 9.06, 9.07, 9.08, 9.09, 9.1, 9.11, 9.12, 9.13, 9.14, 9.15, 9.16, 9.17, 9.18, 9.19, 9.2, 9.21, 9.22, 9.23, 9.24, 9.25, 9.26, 9.27, 9.28, 9.29, 9.3, 9.31, 9.32, 9.33, 9.34, 9.35, 9.36, 9.37, 9.38, 9.39, 9.4, 9.41, 9.42, 9.43, 9.44, 9.45, 9.46, 9.47, 9.48, 9.49, 9.5, 9.51, 9.52, 9.53, 9.54, 9.55, 9.56, 9.57, 9.58, 9.59, 9.6, 9.61, 9.62, 9.63, 9.64, 9.65, 9.66, 9.67, 9.68, 9.69, 9.7, 9.71, 9.72, 9.73, 9.74, 9.75, 9.76, 9.77, 9.78, 9.79, 9.8, 9.81, 9.82, 9.83, 9.84, 9.85, 9.86, 9.87, 9.88, 9.89, 9.9, 9.91, 9.92, 9.93, 9.94, 9.95, 9.96, 9.97, 9.98, 9.99

Game Board © Tarquin Photocopiable under licence – for terms see page 2

Double Double Cross

Focus

Double Double Cross is a game for two or three players which practices doubling and halving numbers to one or two decimal places.

What you need

▶ Playing cards (tens and picture cards removed)
▶ Double Double Cross game board
▶ Coloured pencil crayons / felt tips

▶ How to play

When the tens and picture cards have been removed from the pack the remaining cards are shuffled and placed in a pile, face-down between both players. Player 1 begins by turning two cards from the top of the pack and placing them face-up with a counter between them to make a decimal number. They must then double or halve the number they have chosen.

For example

Player 1 turns over the following cards and can then use them to make any decimal number calculation such as those below.

| Double 6.8 = 13.6 | Halve 6.8 = 3.4 |
| Double 8.6 = 17.2 | Halve 8.6 = 4.3 |

Player 2 checks the calculation and if correct Player 1 can mark the position of that number on the number line with a coloured cross. Player 2 then takes two cards, a five and a three as shown here. So Player 2 has to double or halve three point five or five point three and mark the position of that answer on the number line.

Double 3.5 = 7.0   Halve 3.5 = 1.75
Double 5.3 = 10.6   Halve 5.3 = 2.65

Play continues with players taking two cards, doubling or halving the decimal number they make, and marking the answers on the number line.

How to win

The first player to get four crosses of their own colour together in a line wins the game. The numbers do not need to be consecutive but must not be separated by a cross of the opponent's colour, as shown in the diagram.

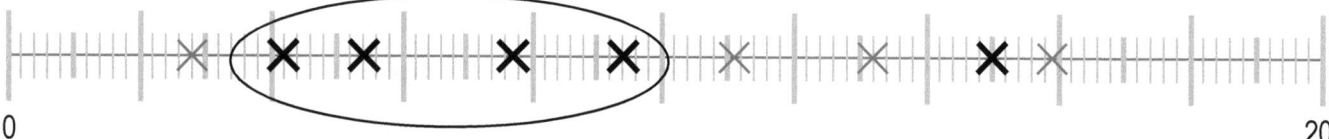

0   20

Rule changes / Next steps

▶ Remove the aces and twos to make larger numbers.
▶ Make links:
double 6.8 = 13.6 **so** double 0.68 = 1.36;
halving 6.8 = 3.4 **so** halving 0.68 = 0.34.
Then play using the 0 – 2 number line, placing the counter in front of the cards to make a number with two decimal places.

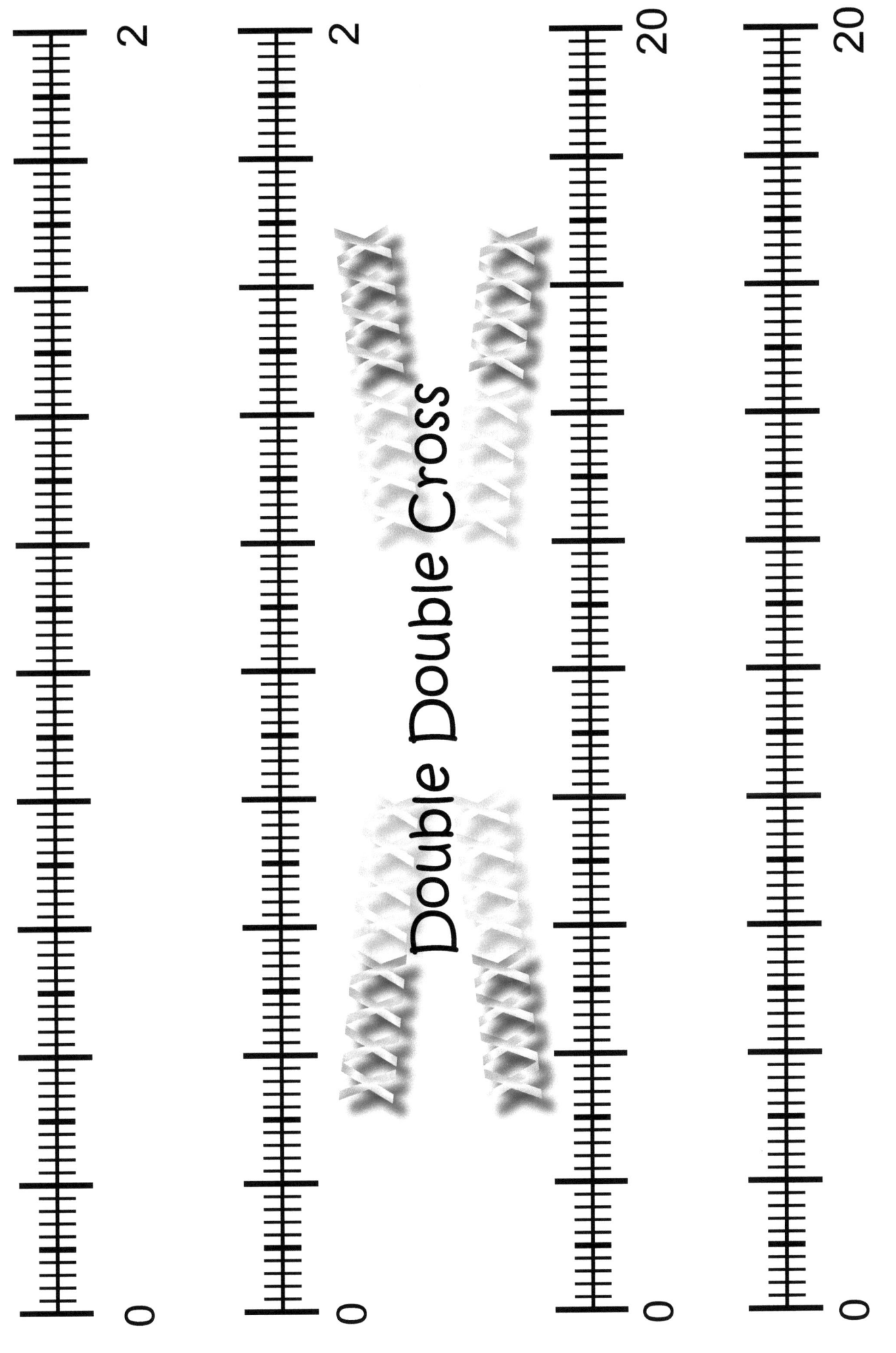

Battle Squares

Focus

Battle Squares is a game for two or more players which practices dividing by one hundred and adding and subtracting numbers to two decimal places.

What you need

- Playing cards (tens and picture cards removed)
- Counters (a different colour for each player)
- Battle Squares game board
- Battle Squares scorecard

How to play

When the tens and picture cards have been removed from the pack the remaining cards are shuffled and placed in a pile, face-down and within reach of all the players.

Player 1 turns over two cards and uses them to make a two-digit number which they then divide by one hundred.

For example

If Player 1 turns over a 3 and a 7 they can either make the number 0.37 or 0.73. They must calculate how much more needs to be added to each number to make one, whilst thinking about how many points they will get for placing a counter on a particular colour.

Player 1 may decide to calculate 0.37 + 0.63 = 1 and put a counter on 0.63 to score 0.5 points for a black square. However, if Player 1 decided to calculate 0.73 + 0.27 = 1 and put a counter on 0.27, they would score one point for a grey square.

Play continues with players taking it in turns to make two-digit numbers, divide them by one hundred, and calculate how many more to make one. They then decide where to place their counters on the board to score the maximum number of points possible (players should watch out for dotty squares, which lose them points). Each player keeps their own score using a scorecard. Players must do all their mental calculations before placing their counter and must also give a correct answer in order to do so.

If a square is already covered by a counter then the player must switch their cards around to make the other two-digit number and must place their counter on the other available square. If both possible squares are covered then the player cannot place a counter but draws two new cards on their next turn. When all the cards have been used, shuffle them and place them in a pile, face-down, ready for the next player's turn.

How to win

The winner of the battle is the player with the most points after an agreed number of rounds.

Rule changes / Next steps

- Do calculations as subtraction from one, such as 1 − 0.54 = 0.46 or 1 − 0.45 = 0.55.
- Players turn over three cards and can use any combination of them to make a two-digit number before dividing it by one hundred.
- Play "in colour" : a full colour downloadable game board and scorecards are available on our website, www.tarquingroup.com.

BATTLE SQUARES

0.01	0.02	0.03	0.04	0.05	0.06	0.07	0.08	0.09	
0.11	0.12	0.13	0.14	0.15	0.16	0.17	0.18	0.19	S
0.21	0.22	0.23	0.24	0.25	0.26	0.27	0.28	0.29	Q
0.31	0.32	0.33	0.34	0.35	0.36	0.37	0.38	0.39	U
0.41	0.42	0.43	0.44	0.45	0.46	0.47	0.48	0.49	A
0.51	0.52	0.53	0.54	0.55	0.56	0.57	0.58	0.59	R
0.61	0.62	0.63	0.64	0.65	0.66	0.67	0.68	0.69	E
0.71	0.72	0.73	0.74	0.75	0.76	0.77	0.78	0.79	S
0.81	0.82	0.83	0.84	0.85	0.86	0.87	0.88	0.89	
	B	A	T	T	L	E			1

Full colour game board and scorecards downloadable from www.tarquingroup.com.

Game Board © Tarquin Photocopiable under licence – for terms see page 2

BATTLE SQUARES SCORECARD

☐ = 0.02 points   ■ = 0.05 points   ▤ = 0.2 points

▨ = 0.1 point   ▦ = -0.09 points

Keep your score like this:

Round Number	Points for square	Total Game points
1	stripes, 0.2 points	0.2
2	dotty, -0.09	0.2 - 0.09 = 0.11
3	grey, 0.1	0.11 + 0.1 = 0.21

Round Number	Points for square	Total Game points
1		
2		
3		
4		
5		
6		
7		
8		
9		
10		
11		
12		
13		
14		
15		

Tower Power

Focus
Tower Power is a game for two or more players which can be used to practice a range of efficient mental methods with numbers up to one hundred.

What you need
▶ Playing cards
▶ Counters

How to play
After shuffling the cards Player 1 deals out seven cards to each player and places the rest of the pack face-down and within reach of all the players. As Player 1 dealt the cards, Player 2 goes first and must turn over two cards from the top of the pack and place them face-up in clear view of everyone. These cards are then used to generate two target numbers for the players to try and make. In making one of the target numbers, players can use any number of cards and any combination of addition, subtraction, multiplication and division.

For example
Player 1 turns over a three and a nine, so the target numbers are thirty-nine and ninety-three. Some possible combinations are as follows:

3 x 11 + 6 = 39   10 x 9 + 2 + 1 = 93   13 x 7 + 2 = 93

Players must place their combinations face-up in front of them for everyone to see and check that they are correct. Each player is allowed to place down as many combinations as they can, as long as they make either target number, but can only use each card once. They then take a counter for each correct calculation they make and use them to start building a tower. After about half a minute to a minute, players pick up all their cards so they still have the same seven cards in their hand for the next turn.

Player 3 then turns over two cards from the pack and the game is repeated for two different target numbers. If one of the cards is a picture card or if both cards have the same value, then replace them with a different card to ensure two target numbers are set. If a player can't find any ways of making the target number they can choose to change any one or two cards from their hand with one or two from the top of the pile. Play continues for five rounds then all the cards are collected, the pack is shuffled, and the players are dealt seven new cards for the game to continue.

How to win
The first player to power up their tower to ten counters is the winner.

Rule changes / Next steps
▶ Allow players to use the same card in more than one calculation.
▶ Use these calculations to show how the equals sign can be used to indicate equivalence, such as 13 x 3 = 7 x 5 + 4 = 39.

End of the Line

Focus

End of the Line is a game for two to four players which can be used to develop a range of efficient mental methods with numbers up to one hundred and fifty.

What you need

- Playing cards
- Counters (a different colour for each player)
- End of the Line game board
- Whiteboard / paper and pen

How to play

Player 1 turns over two cards from the top of the pack and places them next to each other. They must then look to see if they can make multiples of nine by adding, subtracting multiplying or even dividing the numbers on the cards.

For example

Player 1 turns over a seven and a five as shown. Player 1 is not able to make a multiple of nine using these cards. Play passes to Player 2, who turns over another card and tries to make a multiple of nine using any or all three of the numbers on the cards.

With a king, Player 2 can now make a multiple of nine by calculating
13 + 5 = 18   or   13 x 5 + 7 = 72.
Player 2 decides to remove the king and the five from the line and covers the matching multiple of eighteen on the top row of the game board with a counter of their colour.

Player 3 then turns over another card but as it is a ten they are unable to make a multiple of nine, so it becomes the turn of Player 4 to add a card to the line. Player 4 turns over a five and makes a multiple of nine by calculating 7 x 5 + 10 = 45. Player 4 uses all three cards, so removes them and places a counter on forty-five on the game board.

The next player turns over two new cards and starts the line again. Play continues with players taking it in turns to place cards in the line and attempting to make multiples of nine (or whichever muliples are being played) that have not been covered by a counter. A time limit can be set for players to make a multiple and if they can't do it in that time the next player has their turn.

How to win

The winner is the player with the most counters on the line when the last multiple is covered.

Rule changes / Next steps

- Play the game using any of the different sets of multiples on the game board or have a go at playing two different sets of multiples at the same time.
- Allow players to put cards together to make a two-digit number, such as a three and a four to make thirty-four or forty-three.
- Players must make the multiples in the order they come in the line.

| 9 | 18 | 27 | 36 | 45 | 54 | 63 | 72 | 81 | 90 | 99 | 108 |
| 10 | 20 | 30 | 40 | 50 | 60 | 70 | 80 | 90 | 100 | 110 | 120 |

END of the LINE

| 11 | 22 | 33 | 44 | 55 | 66 | 77 | 88 | 99 | 110 | 121 | 132 |
| 12 | 24 | 36 | 48 | 60 | 72 | 84 | 96 | 108 | 120 | 132 | 144 |

Quads

Focus

Quads is a game for three or more players which practices using a range of efficient mental methods for numbers up to ten thousand and to one decimal place.

What you need

▶ Playing cards
▶ Counters (a different colour for each player)
▶ Quads game board

How to play

Player 1 turns over any number of cards and could be asked to add, subtract or multiply them to get an answer depending on what skill or knowledge from the Year 6 programme of study the game is being used to practice. If the player gets the answer correct they can place a counter of their own colour in a circle on the game board.

Player 2 then turns over one or more cards and performs a similar calculation. They can place a counter of their colour onto the game board if the answer is correct, but if they answer incorrectly they are not able to place a counter on that turn. Play continues in this way with players taking it in turns to take one or more cards, answer questions and place counters on the game board.

How to win

The first player to make a Quad is the winner. Quads can be a rectangle or in a straight line (vertical, horizontal or diagonal) as shown in the diagram. Rectangles formed can be small or large and can appear in any orientation.

Remove all the counters and play again.

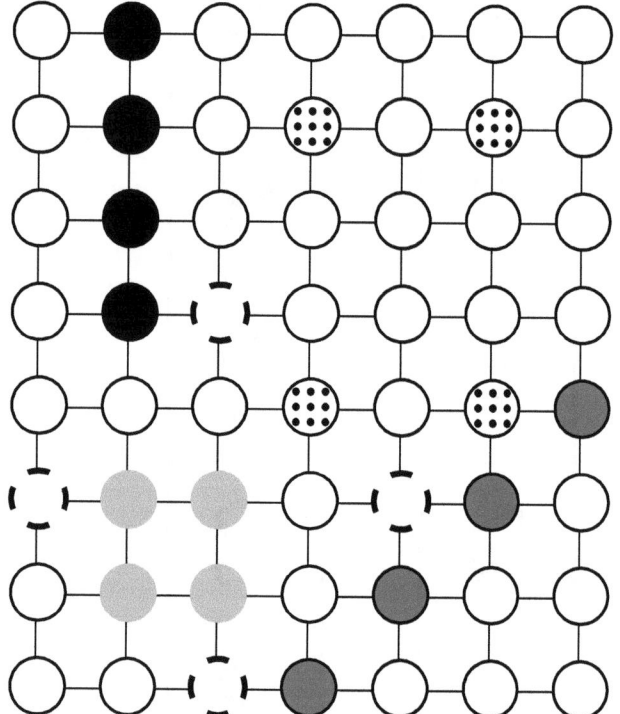

Rule changes / Next steps

▶ Players continue to try and make Quads until all the spaces are covered or until the players agree that no more can be made. Players score four points for every Quad they make and the winner is the player with the most points at the end of the game.

▶ Restrict players to making only rectangles or straight lines to win the game rather than allowing both.

QUADS

Monster Mash-Up

Focus

Monster Mash-up is a game for two to six players which can be used to practice a range of efficient mental methods with numbers up to ten million and to three decimal places.

What you need

▶ Playing cards (cards 1–5)
▶ Counters (one for each player)
▶ Monster Mash-Up game board
▶ Question cards, if using (see Next Steps, below)

How to play

When the cards from six upwards have been removed from the pack the remaining cards are shuffled and placed in a pile, face-down and within reach of all the players. Players then choose a monster and place their counter on it, ready for the start of the game.

Player 1 is asked a question by the question master to practice recall of facts or any skill within the Year 6 programme of study. If answered correctly Player 1 turns over a card and can then move the same number of spaces on the game board. If the answer is incorrect the player is not allowed to move their counter. The other players are then asked questions in turn. If correct they can turn over a card and move the same number of spaces on the game board.

Black holes and transporters

Players must try and avoid the black holes in various positions on the game board, since landing on one sends them back to 'their' monster at the start of the game. However, if a player lands on a black hole containing a symbol, they must transport themselves to any other black hole with the same symbol on it.

Players are allowed to move between tracks and go anywhere on the board, though can't keep moving backwards and forwards from one square to another. If a player lands on top of another counter, the counter landed on is moved back to any monster of that player's choosing.

How to win

The first player to land on or go beyond an end square is the winner.

Rule changes / Next steps

▶ Players can move one bonus square if they can answer a question that another player has answered incorrectly.

▶ Different kinds of question may be selected, dependent, for example, on what a particular child needs to practice, or on particular skills needed for assessment purposes.

▶ Players must turn the exact number to land on an end square and win the game.

▶ Use the set of mixed mental questions provided. Put them face-down on the table for children to pick at random, read aloud and then answer. Alternatively, pass them to an appointed question master to read out.

What is the 3 worth in 4 8<u>3</u>4 263?	What is the value of the underlined digit in <u>6</u> 560 387?	Write the number eight million, nine hundred and four thousand and eighty-four in figures.	Write the number four million and seventeen thousand six hundred and five in figures.
Round 3 487 256 to the nearest million	Round 8.451 to the nearest tenth	What is 35°C colder than 20°C?	The difference between two temperatures is 40°C. One of them is 18°C. What could the other be?
What is six point three divided by one hundred?	What is five point nine multiplied by one thousand?	What number is halfway between three million and eight million?	What is one hundredth subtracted from 0.4?
How many 7p sweets can you buy for £1?	Mum buys two books at 95p each and one book for £1.98. What is the total cost?	What is 1.4 add 1.5 add 1.6?	What is double 37.9?
Twenty times a number is one thousand six hundred. What is the number?	What is one point six multiplied by four?	0.8 x 9 =	600 x 7 =
Seven times a number is three hundred and fifty. What is the number?	What is fifty times thirty times ten?	Which of these numbers are multiples of nine? 67 900 540 209	Which of these numbers is not a multiple of seven? 207 770 84 147
Is 87 a common multiple of 3 and 7? Explain how you know.	What square number is also a multiple of three and nine?	Apart from one, name a common factor of 35 and 84	Apart from one, name a common factor of 63 and 27
Name a prime number between fifty and sixty	What is the nearest prime number to seventy?	Which square number has a digit sum of ten?	Name two factors of thirty-six which have a difference of twelve?

Monster Mash Question Cards © Tarquin Photocopiable under licence – for terms see page 2

6 x (32 ÷ 4) =	20 + 5 x 3 =	8 x 3² =	14 + (9 x 4) = __ − 150
What is five sixths of fifty-four?	What is one fifth of a thousand?	One eighth of a number is 12. What is the number?	I think of a number and find ¾. The answer is 9. What is the number?
True or False? 75% > ⅗	True or False 0.3 < ⅓	What is the decimal equivalent of ⅘ ?	Which of these numbers is nearest to the decimal equivalent of ⅔? 0.3 0.5 0.6 0.7
What is 30% of £120?	What is 10 out of 40 as a percentage?	What is five per cent of five hundred?	6 x __ = 54
½ + ⅜ =	¾ − ⅛ =	⅓ + ¼ =	⅔ − ½ =
If three pens cost £1.20, how much would five pens cost?	Three out of every five children in a class are girls. If there are thirty children in the class, how many are boys?	For every 2 eggs in a recipe you must add 3 spoons of flour. How many spoons of flour must be added with 8 eggs?	Four oranges cost £1.40. How much would three oranges cost?
If $h - 30 = 90$, what is the value of h?	If $t \div 50 = 3$, what is the value of t?	If $a = 8$, what is $4a$?	If $3b = 21$, what is the value of b?
When m has the value of 6, calculate $5m - 7$.	If $40 + 2x = 100$, what is the value of x?	$6w = 28 - w$ $w =$	$4c - 5 = 3c$ $c =$

Tarquin Mathematics Resources

Tarquin has more than a thousand product lines to support and enrich mathematics. You can browse them at **www.tarquingroup.com**.

To make it easy to buy what you need to really use this book, we have some special packages online — put the keyword ACE into the quick search box to see the full range at once.

▶ Packs of Playing Cards - Special ACE prices

▶ Coloured Counters

▶ Beads

Other Tarquin Products designed for you

Books

First Tables Colouring Book

Second Tables Colouring Book

Arithmetic Arithmetic

Tables Cubes

Mathematical Vocabulary 2

The Week's Problem

A Puzzle a Day

Junior Mathematical Team Games

Junior Mini Mathematical Murder Mysteries

Posters

One Million Poster

Multiples Poster

Equal Parts Poster

Quadrilaterals and Polygons Poster

Roman Numerals Poster

Dice and other Manipulatives

Excellent prices on 12-sided and 10-sided dice classroom packs — ideal for mental mathematics.

Tarquin, Suite 74, 17 Holywell Hill, St Albans, AL1 1DT
Tel: +44 (0)1727833866 Fax: +44 (0)845 456 6385
www.tarquingroup.com Follow us on Twitter @TarquinGroup

Printed by Libri Plureos GmbH in Hamburg, Germany